SO
MUCH
WISDOM

CHRISTINA FOYLE

So Much Wisdom

A COMMONPLACE BOOK

ANDRE DEUTSCH

First published 1984 by
André Deutsch Limited
105 Great Russell Street London WC1

Phototypeset by Falcon Graphic Art Ltd.
Wallington, Surrey.
Printed in Great Britain by
Ebenezer Baylis & Son Ltd. Worcester

ISBN 0 233 97568 3

CONTENTS

PREFACE

Being a bookseller's daughter, I have had access to books of all kinds all my life. I cannot remember when I could not read. Very early I found great comfort in my books. I was three years old when the First World War started and saw little of my parents until it was over, as my mother looked after Foyles in the war years; but I had Mrs Molesworth, E. Nesbitt, Peter Pan and Andrew Lang. I began to copy passages that gave me particular pleasure from my books onto cards, and I continued to do so throughout the years.

These words of wisdom have been of enormous comfort and help to me. I read my cards all the time, and they have given me courage to face many catastrophes through a long, exciting life. Without them the war and the blitz on London, near bankruptcy, family tragedy, the vicious onslaughts of wreckers against Foyles – all these would have been far more difficult to bear and overcome.

I do not necessarily agree with all the quotations, but many of them make me laugh, and that is always a good thing to do. I hope that these passages, both light-hearted and serious, collected from books written throughout the ages, will give cheer and inspiration to others.

It was not my invariable habit, alas, to note the book's title when I copied out a passage. Often I wrote down only the author's name. Many of the books from which these quotations come could, of course, be identified quite easily, but it would be very difficult for anyone to trace all of them. I certainly cannot – the quotations have been collected over such a very long time, from such a wide variety of sources. Sometimes, I am sure, the words which struck me were already being quoted by someone else when I first encountered them, and were not found in a book by the person who first said them. If I had been thinking of compiling a book I would naturally have been more methodical, but that thought never entered my head until it was put there, very recently, by friends. I hope readers will forgive me, therefore, if a good deal of my collection of wisdom is passed on as it exists on my cards, as though these profound or useful or inspiring or amusing words had simply been said to me by their authors. That, after all, is how I have always taken them.

Christina Foyle

BOOKS AND THE
PURSUIT OF
KNOWLEDGE

'Bookshops are centres of civilisation. They are the last stand we are all putting up', declared Dame Rebecca West, opening the new bookshop, Branden Books, in Chapel Place, Tunbridge Wells. 'There is a permanent wealth tax being imposed on civilisation called television,' she said. 'There you see actors acting beautifully in worthless plays and you hear political arguments that are inferior to those you would read in any recognised book. The private reader is the buttress against the total ruin of civilisation. He buys books and reads them slowly, often and well.'

Dame Rebecca West
(in a newspaper article)

There is more treasure in books than in all the pirate's loot on Treasure Island. . . and best of all, you can enjoy these riches every day of your life.

Walt Disney

When I get a little money, I buy books; and if any is left, I buy food and clothes.

Erasmus

11

My love of reading I regard as my crowning mercy from God.

Marie Belloc Lowndes

We are going now to the British Museum to read – a fearful way of getting knowledge. If I had Aladdin's lamp I should certainly use it to get books served up to me at a moment's notice.

George Eliot

Anthony Trollope said, with pardonable exaggeration, that 'the habit of reading is the only enjoyment in which there is no alloy; it lasts when all other pleasures fade.'

Speech, 7 December 1868

I can see myself now curled up in all odd corners of the rectory reading *Waverley, Ivanhoe, Rob Roy, Guy Mannering, Old Mortality,* and the rest of them, curled up and entranced so that I was deaf and gave no answer when they called me, and had to be roused to life, which meant tea – with a loud and repeated summons. But what can they say who have been in fairyland? Notoriously, it is impossible to give any true report of its ineffable marvels and delights. Happiness, said De Quincey on his discovery of the paradise that he thought he had found in opium, could be sent down by mail-coach; more truly I could announce my discovery that delight could be contained in small octavos and small type, in a bookshelf three feet long.

Arthur Machen,
Far Off Things

'As soon as you learn to read, you will not see anything again quite as it is. It will all the time be altered by what you have read, and you will never be quite alone again.'

Rumer Godden,
quoted in Iris Origo, *Images and Shadows*

'Talent is a long patience. . .' It is a matter of considering long and attentively what you want to express, so that you may discover an aspect of it that has never before been noticed or reported. There is a part of everything that remains unexplored, for we have fallen into the habit of remembering, whenever we use our eyes, what people before us have thought of the thing we are looking at. Even the slightest thing contains a little that is unknown. We must find it. To describe a blazing fire, or a tree in a plain, we must remain before that fire, or tree, until they no longer resemble for us any other tree or any other fire. That is the way to become original.

Gustave Flaubert

It is not at all suitable for people of great quality to be very learned, but highly necessary for them to know the world and be able to deal with people, and they can't learn that from books but only from experience.

Liselotte, sister-in-law of Louis XIV,
Letters

The best thing for disturbances of the spirit [says Merlyn to his pupil] is to learn. That is the only thing that never fails. You may grow old and trembling in your anatomies, you may lie awake at night listening to the disorder in your veins, you may miss your only love and lose your moneys to a monster, you may see the world about you devastated by evil lunatics, or know your honour trampled in the sewers of baser minds. There is only one thing for it then — to learn.

Learn why the world wags and what wags it. That is the only thing which the mind can never exhaust, never alienate, never be tortured by, never fear or distrust, and never dream of regretting. Learning is the thing for you. Look at what a lot of things there are to learn — pure science, the only purity there is. You can learn astronomy in a lifetime, natural history in three, literature in six. And then, after you have exhausted a milliard lifetimes in biology and medicine and theo-criticism and geography and history and economics, why, you can start to make a cart wheel out of the appropriate wood, or spend fifty years learning to begin to learn to beat your opponent at fencing. After that you can start again on mathematics, until it is time to learn to plough.

T.H. White,
The Sword in the Stone

15

To spend too much time in studies is sloth.

Francis Bacon,
Essays: Of Studies

Learning is often the enemy of initiative.

Lord Samuel

Hobbes said that if he had been at college as long as other people he should have been as great a blockhead as they – W.C.H.

Michel de Montaigne,
Essays

But I was convinced, even at eighteen, and still am, that university is an absolute load of old rubbish unless you're going into a profession. People say it's a marvellous opportunity to take stock and mature, but you can bloody well mature by getting a job, working like hell, and steaming around the place.

Roald Dahl,
Sunday Express, 'Things I wish I had known at 18'

What unimaginable dreariness there will be when there are neither rich nor poor, when all have been educated, when self-education has ceased. A terrible world to dream of, worse, far worse, in darkness and hopelessness than Dante's lowest circle of hell. The spectres of famine, of the plague, of war, etc, are mild and gracious symbols compared with that menacing figure, Universal Education, with which we are threatened, which has already eunuched the genius of the last five-and-twenty years of the nineteenth century, and produced a limitless abortion in that of future time. Education, I tremble before thy dreaded name.

George Moore,
Conversations in Ebury Street

The intelligences we bring into the world are not the same; some can take education like certain steel which takes an edge, and these find the education they want instinctively; other are dipped into the pot in vain, and these are the many.

George Moore,
Conversations in Ebury Street

'My dear-r-r Mad'm,' he would say to my mother, though he had known her as "Polly" in short skirts, 'the sole reason why I have succeeded in life is that I never had any education. If you cram a boy's head full of other folk's ideas, where's the room for his own when he begins to pick them up?'

W. Graham Robertson,
Time Was

As for the Sitwell brothers, both of them had established a mode of aesthetic existence that completely satisfied my own taste. No detail of their way of life was ugly or humdrum. They managed to give a patina of glamour to a visit to an oculist, a bootshop, or a concert. Each catalogue they received from a wine merchant or a bookseller in their hands became a rare volume. With their aristocratic looks, dignified manners and air of lofty disdain, they seemed to me above criticism.

Cecil Beaton,
The Wandering Years: Diaries (1928: Introduction)

RULES OF CONDUCT

There are two things to aim at in this life; first to get what you want; and, after that, to enjoy it. Only the wisest of mankind achieve the second.

Logan Pearsall Smith,
Afterthoughts

Set not thy foot to make the blind to fall;
  Nor wilfully offend they weaker brother;
Nor wound the dead with thy tongue's bitter gall,
  Neither rejoice thou in the fall of other.

Robert Burton,
Anatomy of Melancholy

Remember there is nothing stable in human affairs; therefore avoid undue elation in prosperity, or undue depression in adversity.

Socrates

Cherish the body and you will cherish the soul. That was the belief of the Greeks: the belief in wearing away the body by penance in order that the quivering soul might be exposed had not yet entered the world.

E.M. Forster,
The Longest Journey

I did the same by my meat, as well in regard to quantity as to quality, accustoming myself never to cloy my stomach with eating or drinking, but constantly rise from table with a disposition to eat and drink still more. In this I conformed to the proverb which says that a man, to consult his health, must check his appetite.

Luigi Cornaro,
How To Live One Hundred Years

Against melancholy he [Johnson] recommended constant occupation of mind, a great deal of exercise, moderation in eating and drinking, and especially to shun drinking at night. He said melancholy people were apt to fly to intemperance for relief, but that it sunk them much deeper in misery.

James Boswell,
Life of Johnson

The great source of independence, the French express in a precept of three words, *'Vivre de peu'*, which I have always very much admired. 'To live upon little' is the great security against slavery; and this precept extends to dress and other things beside food and drink.

William Cobbett,
*Advice to Young Men and (Incidentally)
to Young Women, in the Middle and
Higher Ranks of Life*

I always went to bed at least for one hour as early as possible in the afternoon. By this means I was able to press a day and a half's work into one. Nature had not intended mankind to work from eight in the morning to midnight without the refreshment of blessed oblivion which, even if it lasts only twenty minutes, is sufficient to renew all vital forces.

Sir Winston Churchill

Do not expose your private affairs, feelings or inner-most thoughts in public. You are knocking down the walls of your house when you do.

Emily Post,
Etiquette

Do what thy manhood bids thee do,
from none but self expect applause;
He noblest lives and noblest dies
who makes and keeps his self made laws.

Burton
The Kasidah

When asked by a disciple if there were one single word which could serve as a principle of conduct for life, Confucius replied 'Perhaps the word "reciprocity" will do.'

Confucius,
Analects

24

Though a seeker since my birth
Here is all I've learned on earth.
This the gist of what I know:
Give advice and buy a foe.
Random truths are all I find
Stuck like burs about my mind.
Salve a blister. Burn a letter.
Do not wash a cashmere sweater.
Tell a tale, but seldom twice.
Give a stone before advice.

Pressed for rules and verities,
All I recollect are these:
Feed a cold to starve a fever,
Argue with no true believer.
Think-too-long is never-act,
Scratch a myth and find a fact.
Stitch in time saves twenty stitches.
Give the rich, to please them, riches.
Give to love your hearth and hall.
But do not give advice at all.

Phyllis McGinley,
'A Garland of Precepts'

But all these things, *pastiche*, good clothes, vitality, love of adventure, lively interests, must fail, unless one waves over them the magic wand of self-control and a cheerful attitude towards life. Nothing ages a woman like worry or a bad temper. I try always to be an optimist. I refrain from discussing my troubles. A cushion which accompanies me everywhere on my travels explains my philosophy. On it is embroidered, 'Never complain, never explain.'

Elsie de Wolfe (Lady Mendl),
After All

If your nose is close to the grindstone
And you hold it there long enough
In time you'll say there's no such thing
As brooks that babble and birds that sing
These three will all your world compose
Just you, the stone and your poor old nose.

From a two hundred-year-old stone
in a country cemetery

Thy friend has a friend, and thy friend's friend has a friend. Be discreet.

The Talmud

Lastly, if you do resolve to undertake anything of the nature your friends recommend, keep it (if possible) an inpenetrable secret that you are even about such work. Let it be all your own till it is finished entirely in your own way; it will be time enough then to consult such friends as you think capable of judging and advising. If you suffer anyone to interfere till then, 'tis ten to one 'tis the worse for it – it won't be all of a piece. In these cases generally the more cooks, the worse broth, and I have more than once observed those pieces that have stole privately into the world, without midwives, or godfathers and godmothers – like your own, and the Tale of a Tub, and a few others, have far exceeded any that followed.

Your loving daddy,

S.C.

Dr Crisp to Fanny Burney

Be civil to all; sociable to many; familiar with few.

Benjamin Franklin,
Poor Richard's Almanac

She said Kenneth Clark made the mistake of depreciating his own scholarship. This surprised me. 'Yes,' she repeated, 'I have advised him not to be so diffident, or people will cease to respect him.' She said, 'Supreme self-confidence is the essential quality if one is to achieve anything; and one must be an expert on at least one subject, or another.'

Emerald Cunard to James Lees Milne,
quoted in *Prophesying Peace*

I don't ask you to be unafraid – simply to act unafraid.

Gordon of Khartoum

We must see that nothing takes us by surprise and since it is invariably unfamiliarity that makes a thing more formidable than it really is, this habit of continual reflection will ensure that no form of adversity finds you a complete beginner.

Seneca,
Letters from a Stoic

Never go out to meet trouble. If you will just sit still, nine cases out of ten someone will intercept it before it reaches you.

Calvin Coolidge

Nothing, to my way of thinking, is better proof of a well ordered mind than a man's ability to stop just where he is and pass some time in his own company.

Seneca,
Letters from a Stoic

It is my belief, you might call it my philosophy, that in this life you don't achieve simplicity, or preserve it when you are fortunate enough to acquire it, unless you deliberately bar from your way of life, your everyday existence, anything that is phoney. I liked a simple life, I had no pretensions and I didn't want to fool anybody. I liked to be frank and I had got far enough in my life to feel that I didn't need to pretend that I was other than I was.

Lord Thomson,
After I was Sixty

If you can keep your head while those about you are losing theirs, perhaps you do not understand the situation.

Nelson Boswell,
Successful Living Day by Day

'. . . . practical old Party suggests that if he takes . . . good enough care of his laundry, his soul will . . . take care of itself.' He raises a warning finger and adds, 'But never the other way about!'

Somerset Maugham

The most valuable thing I have learned from life is to regret nothing. Life is short, nature is hostile, and man is ridiculous. But oddly enough, most misfortunes have their compensations, and with a certain humour and a good deal of horse sense, one can make a fairly good job of what is, after all, a matter of very small consequence.

Somerset Maugham

Always do what you please, and send everybody to Hell, and take the consequences. Damned Good Rule of Life.

Norman Douglas

This disaster – and believe me, it seemed at the time a disaster of the first magnitude – taught me a lesson I have never forgotten. If you intend to break a rule or regulation, never ask first if you can do it. Break it. If you ask first you are practically committing two offences instead of one.

Lord Brabazon,
The Brabazon Story

'A man should be careful never to tell tales of himself to his own disadvantage. People may be amused and laugh at the time, but they will be remembered and brought out against him upon some subsequent occasion.'

Johnson in James Boswell
Life of Johnson

Regard him that speaks ill of you, when you are innocent, more worthy of forgiveness than him who carried the report of it to you.

Kai Ka'us Ibn Iskander,
A Mirror for Princes

Airy nonchalance is a supreme form of astuteness, and not seldom the highest rewards go the childlike and irresponsible. The great *enjoy* protecting the scatter-brains, for the simple reason that they seem to stand in need of protection.

André Maurois,
Victor Hugo

Finally, a soft voice commands closer attention than does a loud voice. People will hang on your every word only if they have to in order to catch every word. This is something that Mafia dons have long known.

Quentin Crisp and Donald Carroll,
Doing it with Style

Also remember constantly this rule: the more you think for yourself, the more marked will your individuality be.

George Bernard Shaw,
My Dear Dorethea

Half blind with shame, half choked with dirt,
Man cannot tell, but Allah knows
How much the other side was hurt!

Rudyard Kipling,
'Boxing', from *Verses on Games*

'The last two lines, illustrate my favourite military maxim, that when things are going badly in battle, the best tonic is to take one's mind off one's own troubles by considering what a rotten time one's opponent must be having.'

Field-Marshall Earl Wavell,
Other Men's Flowers

In the meantime cling tooth and nail to the following rule: not to give in to adversity, never to trust prosperity, and always take full note of fortune's habit of behaving just as she pleases, treating her as if she were actually going to do everything it is in her power to do. Whatever you have been expecting for some time comes as less of a shock.

Seneca
Letters from a Stoic

'My dear fellow,' said Labby, 'where would you have been if you had not been persistently maligned? You owe your position to these attacks. But take my advice: never reply to them, never correct mis-statements. If you try to brush away the filth, you will only soil your own hands.'

Hesketh Pearson,
Labby

Listen. Say less rather than more. If you want to be smart, play stupid!

Helena Rubenstein,
My Life for Beauty

We went back to England together. When we arrived at the customs shed, Syrie said: 'Always choose the oldest customs' official. No chance of promotion.'

Somerset Maugham,
quoting his wife

'My dear Caddy,' said Mr Jellyby. 'Never have . . .'

'Not Prince, Pa?' faltered Caddy. 'Not have Prince?'

'Yes, my dear,' said Mr Jellyby. 'Have him, certainly. But never have . . .'

I mentioned in my account of our first visit in Thavies Inn, that Richard described Mr Jellyby as frequently opening his mouth after dinner without saying anything. It was a habit of his. He opened his mouth now, a great many times, and shook his head in a melancholy manner.

'What do you wish me not to have? Don't have what, dear Pa?' asked Caddy, coaxing him, with her arms round his neck.

'Never have a Mission, my dear child.'

Charles Dickens,
Bleak House

OCCUPATION
AND
IDLENESS

Start, I beseech you, with a conviction firmly fixed on your mind, that you have no right to live in this world; that, being of hale body and sound mind, you have no right to any earthly existence, without doing work of some sort or another, unless you have ample fortune whereon to live clear of debt; and, that even in that case, you have no right to breed children to be kept by others, or to be exposed to the chance of being so kept.

William Cobbett,
Advice to Young Men . . .

The happy people are those who are producing something; the bored people are those who are consuming much and producing nothing. . . . Boredom then, is a certain sign that we are allowing our faculties to rust in idleness. When people are bored, they generally look about for a new pleasure, or take a holiday. There is no greater mistake: what they want is some hard piece of work, some productive drudgery. Doctors are fond of sending their fashionable patients to take a rest cure. In nine cases out of ten a work cure would do them far more good.

Dean Inge,
Wit and Wisdom

And this is the true cause that so many great men, ladies and gentlewomen, labour of this disease in country and city; for idleness is an appendix to nobility; they count it a disgrace to work, and spend all their days in sports, recreations and pastimes, and will therefore take no pains, be of no vocation; they feed liberally, fare well, want exercise, action, employment (for to work, I say, they may not abide), and company to their desires, and thence their bodies become full of gross humours, wind, crudities, their minds disquieted, dull, heavy, etc.; care, jealousy, fear of some diseases, sullen fits, weeping fits, seize too familiarly on them. For what will not fear and phantasy work in an idle body? What distempers will they not cause? When the children of Israel murmured against Pharoah in Egypt, he commended his officers to double their task, and let them get straw themselves, and yet make their full number of bricks; for the sole cause why they mutiny, and are evil at ease, is, 'they are idle'.

Robert Burton,
Anatomy of Melancholy

He acknowledged to himself that this was the real happy life he had long desired and wished for, and had foolishly let himself be seduced away from it by a senseless and vain ambition, which had only brought trouble to himself and others; that highest good which he had thought to obtain by arms and fleets and soldiers he had now discovered unexpectedly in idleness, leisure and repose. As, indeed, what other end or period is there of all the wars and dangers which hapless princes run into, whose misery and folly it is, not merely that they make luxury and pleasure, instead of virtue and excellence, the object of their lives, but that they do not so much as know where this luxury and pleasures are to be found?

Plutarch,
Life of Demetrius

The one important thing I have learnt over the years is the difference between taking one's work seriously and taking oneself seriously. The first is imperative – the second disastrous.

Margot Fonteyn,
Margot Fonteyn

For this reason it is that I complain of our laws, not that they keep us too long to our work, but that they set us to work too late. For the frailty of life considered, and to how many ordinary and natural rocks it is exposed, one ought not to give up so large a portion of it to childhood, idleness, and apprenticeship. Which Cotton thus renders: 'Birth though noble, ought not to share so large a vacancy, and so tedious a course of education.'

Michel de Montaigne,
Essays

AMBITION
AND
ACHIEVEMENT

When King Pyrrhus prepared for his expedition into Italy, his wise counsellor Cyneas, to make him sensible of the vanity of his ambition: 'Well, sir,' said he, 'to what end do you make all this mighty preparation?' 'To make myself master of Italy,' replied the King. 'And what after that is done?' said Cyneas. 'I will pass over into Gaul and Spain,' said the other. 'And what then?' 'I will then go to subdue Africa; and lastly, when I have brought the whole world to my subjection, I will sit down and rest content at my own ease.' 'For God sake, sir,' replied Cyneas, 'tell me what hinders that you may not,if you please, be now in the condition you speak of? Why do you not now at this instant, settle yourself in the state you seem to aim at, and spare all the labour and hazard you interpose?'

Michel de Montaigne,
Essays

Anyone who wants to get to the top has to have the guts to be hated. That applies to politicians, writers, anybody who gets into a certain position. Because that's how you get there. You don't get there by everybody loving you. Everybody in the world wants to be liked by everybody else. That's human nature. But you have to learn to take it.

Bette Davis,
The Lonely Life

45

'People are always blaming their circumstances for what they are', Vivie exclaims in contempt and disgust. 'I don't believe in circumstances. The people who get on in this world are the people who get up and look for the circumstances they want, and, if they can't find them, make them.' She may be forgiven much for that valiant remark.

St John Ervine,
Bernard Shaw: His Life, Work and Friends

The pursuit of social success, in the form of prestige or power or both, is the most important obstacle to happiness in a competitive society. I am not denying that success is an ingredient in happiness – to some, a very important ingredient. But it does not, by itself, suffice to satisfy most people. You may be rich and admired, but if you have no friends, no interests, no spontaneous useless pleasures, you will be miserable. Living for social success is one form of living by a theory, and all living by theory is dusty and desiccating.

Bertrand Russell,
Portraits from Memory and Other Essays

I try to make friends wherever I go and it is my fond belief that I usually succeed. The way I look at it, everyone has an idea and one in a dozen may be a good idea. If you have to talk to a dozen people to get one good idea, even just a glimmering of an idea, that isn't wasteful work. People are continually passing things on to me because I have given them to believe that I will be interested; I might even pay for it! Sometimes, usually when it is least expected, something comes up that is touched with gold.

Lord Thomson,
After I was Sixty

Now listen, good friend Morley; moral force is a fine thing, especially in speculation, and so is a community of goods, especially when a man has no property, but when you have lived as long as I have, and have tasted of the world's delights, you'll comprehend the rapture of acquisition, and learn that it is generally secured by very coarse means.

Benjamin Disraeli,
Sybil

He that piles up treasure has much to lose.

Lao-Tzu,
Tao-te-ching

Because the good old rule
  Sufficeth them, the simple plan,
That they should take, who have the power,
  And they should keep who can.

Wordsworth,
Rob Roy's Grave

If you wish in the world to advance
Your merits you're bound to enhance
You must stir it and stump it
And blow your own trumpet
Or trust me, you haven't a chance. . . .

W.S. Gilbert,
Iolanthe

SERENITY
AND
ENJOYMENT

Happiness is nothing more than good health and a bad memory.

Dr Albert Schweitzer

'Dynamic', I said, letting more water into the bath. Wasn't that a mistake on my part? I recalled Max Beerbohm, who sat in the sun on his Rapallo terrace, did nothing, and watched his reputation grow.

Cecil Roberts,
The Bright Twenties

The wine which is poured out first is the purest wine in the bottle, the heaviest particles and any cloudiness settling to the bottom. It is just the same with human life. The best comes first. Are we going to let others drain it so as to keep the dregs for ourselves? Let that sentence stick in your mind, accepted as unquestioningly as if it had been uttered by an oracle: Life's finest days, for us poor human beings, fly first.

Seneca,
Letters from a Stoic

'This is the true joy of life,' . . . 'the being a force of Nature instead of a feverish little clod of ailments and grievances complaining that the world will not devote itself to making you happy.'

George Bernard Shaw,
Preface to *Man and Superman*

Temperance, says one of the ancients, is the best contriver of pleasure – temperance which produces health of body and mind, and keeps one in a state of calm and restrained happiness. One has no need of artificial aids or shows or expense in order to procure enjoyment. Some little game which is invented, something read, a task undertaken, a walk, an artless conversation which refreshes after work, make one enjoy a more real happiness, than the most alluring music.

Fénelon,
The Education of Girls

The real thing in life, is to be happy. The older I get the more convinced I am that no ambition is worth pursuing except that of being rather happier than other men. Fame of any kind is only of use insofar as it leads to this, even the fame of being a poet which is perhaps more satisfactory and lasting than the rest. I would not give a brass button to be the greatest general that ever won a battle or even I think the greatest statesman that ever bamboozled the world. But I should like to be quite happy to the last day of my life, and to be able to inspire affection at the age of eighty, as I believe Goethe is said to have done.

Wilfred Scawen Blunt,
in a letter to George Wyndham

On the whole I would say that fame helps slightly more towards happiness than towards unhappiness. As a means towards felicity I would rank it about equal with money. And about equal with good health. And about equal with a clear conscience. And far lower than a steady reciprocated affection for a person of the opposite sex. And far higher than passionate love. I shall be contradicted. But I am a realist, not a sentimentalist.

Arnold Bennett,
Sketches for an Autobiography

With more money to spend and more leisure in which to spend it they tend to move their bodies from one place to another at a greater speed, but this does not mean that they are being more useful or that they are enjoying themselves. They have merely been caught up in the feverish race of modern living. The treadmills turn faster and faster but they are still treadmills. Only those who have the desire and courage to jump off know what it is to see the whole thing for the farce it is.

Patience Strong

It's rather odd really, how living in this place absolutely alone, after having more people here . . . I would hate to have anyone here. It's wonderfully dreamy to be in a house to oneself. One can wander round from room to room; you can sleep in a different room every night. . . . You pay the price in a way, but it's better to be too lonely than too much with people you don't like. The worse thing in life is to be at close company with people you don't like very much.

Stevie Smith
quoted by Kay Dick in *Ivy and Stevie:*
Conversations with
Ivy Compton-Burnett and Stevie Smith

Let me return to the topic of the happiness of fools. After a life lived out in much jollity, with no fear of death, or sense of it, they go straight to the Elysian Fields, there to entertain the pious and idle shades with their jests. Let us go about, then, and compare the lot of the wise man with that of the fool. Fancy some pattern of wisdom to put up against him, a man who wore out his whole boyhood and youth in pursuing the learned disciplines. He wasted the pleasantest time of life in unintermitted watchings, cares, and studies; and through the remaining part of it he never tasted so much as a tittle of pleasure; always frugal, impecunious, sad, austere; unfair and strict towards himself, morose and unamiable to others; afflicted by pallor, leanness, invalidism, sore eyes, premature age and white hair; dying before his appointed day. By the way, what difference does it make when a man of that sort dies? He has never lived. There you have a clear picture of the wise man.

Erasmus,
Praise of Folly

In fact, he taught that the supreme goal is the happiness which comes from peace of mind, achieved by banishing fear of the gods and fear of death, and by avoiding immediate pleasures that are outweighed by greater consequent pains.

Epicurus,
Morals

Three ducks on a pond
The blue sky beyond,
White clouds on the wing,
What a little thing,
To remember for years,
To remember with tears.

W. Graham Robertson,
Time Was

Hearing this, Tseng Hsi put down his zither and rose to reply. 'My dream is a simple one. I would like it to be the end of springtime. I would like to be dressed in fresh light clothes. Then I would like to go with some friends and swim in the river Yi and cool in the spring breezes. After we had swum for a while, I dream of our returning slowly home, talking and singing along the way.'

Confucius looked at Tseng Hsi for a moment, then smiled. 'You know, all the dreams I have heard have merit. But if I were to choose myself to accompany one of you, it would be you, Tseng Hsi.'

Confucius,
Analects

When you draw on a goose-down sleeping-bag, you understand how wild animals survive in their coats of fur during an arctic winter. You have no need of artificial heat; within minutes the down itself seems warm, as though it were transferring energy to you instead of you to it. In a sleeping-bag, after an ember-cooked meal, you feel free of civilization's elaborate accoutrements and realize the basic simplicity of life. The only essentials are a covering for your body, a shelter from the weather and a little food. For the night, at least, you can forget all else. God made life simple. It is man who complicates it.

Charles Lindbergh

Of a sane man there is only one safe definition. He is a man who can have tragedy in his heart and comedy in his head.

G.K. Chesterton,
Tremendous Trifles

What a fine lesson is conveyed to the mind – to take no note of time but by its benefits, to watch only for the smiles and neglect the frowns of fate, to compose our lives of bright and gentle moments, turning always to the sunny side of things, and letting the rest slip from our imaginations, unheeded or forgotten.

William Hazlitt

THE CONDUCT
OF A
BUSINESS

In business, it will be remembered, his belief was that 'there can be no permanent success unless the head be an autocrat – of course the more disguised by the silken glove the better'. All his working life he had, in fact, been an autocrat and had taken all vital decisions himself.

Said of
The First Lord Cowdray

There is nothing that can ever take the place of cash. The overwhelming majority of business problems (and so many recent business failures) result from businessmen extending themselves too far. There is most definitely a place – and a need – for the use of credit in business. However, I have always believed that the businessman who uses credit the most sparingly is the one who has the greatest chance for achieving success.

Paul Getty,
How to be Rich

Never over-extend yourself and risk the whole enterprise. Far better to stay in your small premises and work long hours than to put yourself in debt to backers and banks. Otherwise you will find that even if the business continues to exist, you are no longer in control.

Princess Beris Randaouroff,
The Art of Living

I therefore said what was true as far as it went, that if I had my time over again I would never exchange independence for a partnership, however attractive it might appear.

Percy Muir,
Minding my Own Business

... and he (a merchant) should never do business with close friends. If he does, he must abandon any desire for profit if he wishes to prevent the friendship from being destroyed, for many a friendship has been terminated by reason of some trifle of profit or loss.

Kai Ka'us Ibn Iskander,
A Mirror for Princes

I have no doubt you will get through the business very well, Mr Hoaxem, particularly if you be 'frank and explicit'; that is the right line to take when you wish to conceal your own mind and to confuse the minds of others. Good morning!

Benjamin Disraeli,
Sybil

Nobody was ever meant
To remember or invent
What he did with every cent.

Robert Frost

Yet do not tie the tax gatherer's hands completely, for if you begrudge the fire a little fat, your grill will remain uncooked, and unless you leave a farthing for others, you will not be able to enjoy your shilling. If you are avaricious, those who have been disappointed will not preserve silence nor allow the facts to remain hidden.

Kai Ka'us Ibn Iskandar,
A Mirror for Princes

There is a danger in the facility with which statistics can be mass-produced nowadays and letters dictated or taped. They become more important than the people or business situations. Statistics become a substitute for experience, a letter a substitute for personal contact, and a memorandum a substitute for decision. Bureaucratic control becomes more important than action.

Lord Marks,
of Marks and Spencer

'Our men are not experts,' said Henry Ford. 'We have most unfortunately found it necessary to get rid of a man as soon as he thinks himself an expert. The moment one gets into the expert state of mind a great number of things become impossible. Our new operations are always directed by men who have no previous knowledge of the subject and, therefore, have not had a chance to get on really familiar terms with the impossible.'

The Wild Wheel –
The World of Henry Ford

The majority is by no means omniscient just because it is the majority. In fact, I've found that the line which divides majority opinion from mass hysteria is often so fine as to be virtually invisible. This holds as true in business as it does in any other aspect of human activity.

Paul Getty,
How to be Rich

The fatal fact about nepotism is that the really good people won't go to work for you in the first place or will quit or quit trying for your job when they spot your uncle, brother, nephew, wife, mistress, or son on the payroll. They can't expect a fair shake if you're getting breakfast news from a special source.

Robert Townsend,
Up the Organisation

Allen undoubtedly inherited, learnt or imitated John Lane's manner of running a publishing house as if it was a great sport in which he wanted all his colleagues to share. Unfortunately for those colleagues Allen, in this unlike John Lane, changed the rules – and the team – as often as possible. And, unfortunately for those who would wish to hold up John Lane's loyalty to his subordinates as a model, Allen's methods proved, in almost every worldly sense, far more successful.

J.E. Morpurgo,
Allen Lane: King Penguin

Hiring: to keep an organization young and fit, don't hire anyone until everybody's so overworked they'll be glad to see the newcomer no matter where he sits.

Robert Townsend,
Up the Organisation

'Slow down,' he advised. 'This job should take two weeks.'

'But how can I stretch two days' work into two weeks?'

'Easy. It just takes a little experience. Hide behind the shelves. Do a little reading each day, or take a nap on an empty shelf. We can hear anyone coming down the metal staircase.'

There was no choice. I was outnumbered. I converted an empty shelf into a desk, on which I read books (no shortage to choose from) or wrote poetry. It furthered my education and nobody came to check on us in the entire two weeks. I began to feel that no one knew we existed, that we had been banished to a sort of nether world like disfavoured gods.

I had learned my first lesson as an apprentice bookseller: Never leave employees alone and presume they're working.

H.P. Kraus (world-famous antiquarian bookseller),
A Rare Book Saga

MONEY

However, he did but justify the saying of Plato that the only certain way to be truly rich is not to have more property, but fewer desires. For whoever is always grasping at more avows that he is still in want, and must be poor in the midst of affluence.

Plutarch,
Life of Demetrius

There are three faithful friends – an old wife, an old dog, and ready money.

Benjamin Franklin,
Poor Richard's Almanac

She was learning what freedoms money conferred when one stopped working for it and allowed it to work for one.

Edmonde Charles Roux,
Chanel and Her World

Money is woman's only bulwark against the world.

Gaby Deslys

Did Titian or Rubens disregard their pecuniary rewards? As far as we know, Shakespeare worked always for money, giving the best of his intellect to support his trade as an actor. In our own century what literary names stand higher than those of Byron, Tennyson, Scott, Dickens, Macaulay, and Carlyle? And I think I may say that none of those great men neglected the pecuniary result of their labours.

Anthony Trollope,
An Autobiography

The most pleasing thing that money can buy is privacy.

Calouste Gulbenkian

You may say that money is a handicap and will not buy anything worth buying. I disagree. The general instinct of mankind to obtain money is a sound instinct. Money is certainly not a handicap. Money will buy nearly everything – except a clear conscience and a cheerful temperament. It will buy comfort. It will buy quite a lot of health.

Arnold Bennett,
Sketches for an Autobiography

After burying into the Consols and the Reduced, I read Seneca 'On the Contempt of Wealth'. What intolerable nonsense! . . . . I have been very poor the greater part of my life, and have borne it as well, I believe, as most people, but I can safely say that I have been happier every guinea I have gained.

Sydney Smith,
quoted in Hesketh Pearson, *Smith of Smiths*

I do not complain of your speaking of my 'enormous and unlimited wealth' though as a matter of fact it is not enormous, and I have never had any difficulty in finding its limits. But what is monstrous is this, that in consequence of what you said, thousands of mendicant pens are being sharpened. The parson's widow, the bedridden Scot born at Delmeny, the author who has long watched my career, the industrious grocer who has been ruined by backing my horses, the poet who has composed a sonnet to the G.O.M., the family that wishes to emigrate – all these and a myriad of others, are preparing for action. Not to speak of the hospital that wants a wing, the roofless church, the club of hearty Liberals in an impoverished district, the football club that wants a patron, the village band that wants instruments, all of which are preparing for the warpath . . . .

Lord Rosebery to Lord Randolph Churchill, 30 June 1886, quoted in Robert Rhodes James, *Lord Randolph Churchill*. Rosebery is complaining of the demands for financial aid which will follow Churchill's mention in an election speech of Rosebery's 'enormous and unlimited wealth'.

'I think', replied Phil, after pensively tracing out a crosswrinkle in his forehead with the brush handle, 'that mischeevious consequences is always meant when money's asked for.'

Phil Squod in Charles Dickens,
Bleak House

POWER
AND
POLITICS

With Plato and Cicero Erasmus affirmed that he only is fit to be a ruler who has no desire to rule.

Roland H. Bainton,
Erasmus of Christendom

Oh, the folly of universal suffrage! The folly of constitutional government! I used to say, 'Surely, a good despot is better than a mob.' But now I'm convinced that a bad despot, even, is better.

Henry Harland

It is the same attitude as one sees over the whole world – blank fatalistic resignation to stupid and wicked governments, to anything or any person with power.

Aldous Huxley

And among those occasions on which people fall below self-interest are most of the occasions on which they are convinced that they are acting from idealistic motives. Much that passes as idealism is disguised hatred or disguised love of power.

Samuel Butler,
Way of All Flesh

I

Men of England, wherefore plough
For the lords who lay ye low?
Wherefore weave with toil and care
The rich robes your tyrants wear?

II

Wherefore feed, and clothe, and save,
From the cradle to the grave,
Those ungrateful drones who would
Drain your seat – nay, drink your blood?

Shelley,
Song to the Men of England

I am no friend of the people. As a force, by which the tenor of the time is conditioned, they inspire me with distrust, with fear; as a visible multitude, they make me shrink aloof, and often move me to abhorrence. For the greater part of my life, the people signified to me the London crowd, and no phrase of temperate meaning would utter my thoughts of them under that aspect. The people as country-folk are little known to me; such glimpses as I have had of them do not invite to nearer acquaintance. Every instinct of my being is anti-democratic, and I dread to think of what our England may become when Demos rules irresistibly.

George Gissing,
The Private Papers of Henry Ryecroft

Furthermore, I have a built-in sympathy for anyone the pack is after; especially when the pack consists of the Intelligentsia – as I know from personal experience, the most malignant, unscrupulous and ferocious of all.

Malcolm Muggeridge

With what aim in view they proceeded to display themselves as the protectors of the poor – always the cry of those who for personal advantage seek to harass and overthrow the government.

Lucy Norton (Ed.),
Duc de Saint-Simon, Memoirs

When the opportunity arose Duff continued: 'Sir Stafford Cripps is a maniac – a righteous man like Robespierre – a menace. By his lust for power he will ruin England. His brother once told me: "If my brother Stafford ever gets to power he will wreck the country, and I'm off." And sure enough, when Stafford became Chancellor of the Exchequer his brother migrated with all his possessions to South Africa. All great good men are a menace: they bring nothing but misery to the world. Gandhi has done more harm than any gangster. Gangsters only work in small ways. They murder old women and orphans – but what else are old women and orphans for but to be ill-treated?'

Duff Cooper

The British are bad at anger; but it's an emotion they'll have to learn. We're only going to temper juvenile brutality, union irresponsibility, the fiscal predatoriness of government and the insolence of bureaucracy by getting angry.

Anthony Burgess

'A Politician', said Oscar Wilde, 'is a man who approaches every question with an open mouth.'

Oscar Wilde

Bennett, in company for a weekend at Beaverbrook's with two of the most celebrated political leaders of the day, discovered from their conversation that they were more concerned with the ruin of their opponents than with the good of the country. In the natural simplicity and kindness of his heart he had never imagined such cynicism to be possible. Wishing to be thought unshockable, he made no comment to others; but to myself he confided that he had been horrified.

Frank Swinnerton,
Arnold Bennett: A Last Word

'I note from my morning paper today, that you have called the Tories "a lot of boneheads". Why pick on the Tories particularly? Surely, *all* politicians are boneheads? Otherwise they would not be politicians. I am a Liberal myself, that is to say, I have no particular political creed except that most politicians are scoundrels, and the majority of them are only out for what they can get for themselves and don't really care one hoot in Hell for the countries of which they are, were, or would like to be Dictators.

Best wishes as always,
from Vyvyan [Holland].

Compton Mackenzie,
My Life and Times

Indeed, the leading part that business plays – and pays – as a financier of governments and their spending programmes is very often overlooked or ignored. By a coincidence in no way odd, the blindest eye is usually turned by those politicians who are the most strident business-baiters. They see business as a limitless bonanza from which public revenue may be mined without end or limit – and do not hesitate to legislate accordingly.

Paul Getty,
How to be Rich

When two or three respectable citizens were given government posts, he reached this dismal conclusion: 'I cannot help looking upon it as a most melancholy proof of the miserable state of this country when men of integrity and ability are employed. If it was possible to have gone on without them, I am sure they would never have been thought of.'

Sydney Smith,
in Hesketh Pearson, *Smith of Smiths*

No one fights political battles for the sake of peace and quiet; no downright incorruptible idealist could endure the wirepulling, charlatanry, humbug, chicanery, place-seeking, time-serving, and power-snatching, which are the necessary ingredients of politics; and the spectacle of a successful and mainly disinterested statesman, whether right, left or centre, is one that the world awaits in vain.

Hesketh Pearson,
Dizzy [Disraeli]

The English have always been the most taxable of peoples. An American citizen has put it to his representatives in Congress: 'When you get to Washington, don't do anything for me: I can't afford it.' The slogan should be impressed upon the portals of Westminster.

A.L. Rowse.
Portraits and Views

LAW

Thousands of men have injured themselves by resort-
ing to the law; while very few ever bettered themselves
by it, except such resort were unavoidable.

William Cobbett,
Advice to Young Men . . .

The one great principle of the English law is, to make
business for itself. There is no other principle distinctly,
certainly, and consistently maintained through all its
narrow turnings. Viewed by this light it becomes a
coherent scheme, and not the monstrous maze the laity
are apt to think it. Let them but once clearly perceive
that its grand principle is to make business for itself at
their expense, and surely they will cease to grumble.

Charles Dickens,
Bleak House

And Christ's counsel concerning lawsuits was never so
fit to be inculcated as in this age: 'Agree with thine
adversary quickly,' etc. (Matt. v.25).

Robert Burton,
Anatomy of Melancholy

He that goes to law holds a wolf by the ears.

Robert Burton,
Anatomy of Melancholy

There was once a professor of law who said to his students: 'If you have the facts on your side, hammer them into the jury, and if you have the law on your side, hammer it into the judge.'
'But if you have neither the facts nor the law?'
'Then hammer hell into the table.'

Somerset Maugham.

LIBERTY

Nothing is more rooted in my mind than the vast distinction between the individual and the class. Take a man by himself, and there is generally some reason to be found in him, some disposition for good; mass him with his fellows in the social organism, and ten to one he becomes a blatant creature, without a thought of his own, ready for any evil to which contagion prompts him. It is because nations tend to stupidity and baseness that mankind moves so slowly; it is because individuals have a capacity for better things that it moves at all.

In my youth, looking at this man and that, I marvelled that humanity had made so little progress. Now, looking at men in the multitude, I marvel that they have advanced so far.

George Gissing,
The Private Papers of Henry Ryecroft

The masses don't care about freedom (they leave that to unpopular minority-minded dissidents); all the masses care about is wage-increases, i.e. material objects, Bingo-mania, etc. Communist Russia deliberately allows them unlimited drink; in Britain we might say TV is the opium of the people, it is certainly their religion.

A.L. Rowse.
Portraits and Views

Whenever a people, thirsting for liberty, discovers that its leaders will give it whatever it seeks, even to the point of intoxication, then if the Government resists its more extreme demands it is called tyranny, and those who show discipline to their superiors are called lackeys.

The father, filled with fear, comes to treat his son as equal and is no longer respected. The master no longer dares reprimand his servants and is mocked by them. The young claim the same consideration as the old, who in no way wishing to seem severe, yield to them.

In the name of liberty, no one is any longer respected. In the midst of this licence, there grows and flourishes a weed called tyranny.

Plato,
8th Book of *The Republic*

To have a feeling for the liberty enjoyed in other European countries one must have sojourned in that solitude without repose, in that prison without leisure, that is called Russia.

If ever your sons should be discontented with France, try my recipe: tell them to go to Russia. It is a journey useful to every foreigner; whoever has well examined that country will be content to live anywhere else.

Astolphe de Custine,
Russia in 1839

But if the chief imponderable advantage of the communist cult is, as I have hinted, a fanatical hatred of the bourgeois virtues combined with a sensuous abandonment to a feeling of aesthetic superiority, the chief imponderable advantage of British and American Individualism is that magical feeling of being alone with the Secret of Life, alone with the Cosmos, alone with the First Cause, that feeling of independence so dear to Walt Whitman, that sense of being inherently free from the domination of any class, any age, any party, any fashion of thought, free in the midst of the Creation, free in the presence of the Creator, free from any cause but the First Cause, from any order but the Order of Man; free to share, as in honour bound, a due portion of this hard world's labour; free to express upon the affairs of that world our private, personal, individual, exceptional, and often fantastical opinions!

John Cowper Powys

We talked of different forms of government; and it was remarked what difficulties an excess of liberalism presents, as it calls forth the demands of individuals, and, from the quantity of wishes, raises uncertainty as to which should be satisfied. In the long run, over-great goodness, mildness, and moral delicacy, will not do, while underneath there is a mixed and sometimes vicious world to manage and hold in respect.

Goethe,
Conversations with Eckermann

Reduce your requirements to a minimum. In that way, you can preserve your independence and individuality. If you want many material possessions, you can only get them by selling your time, that is, your life to your fellow men. It is not a good bargain. Learn to do without luxuries and you are free. Poor in money but rich in sunny hours and summer days. A man can be wealthy, only in proportion to the number of things he can let alone.

Thoreau,
Walden, 2, Where I Lived and What I Lived For

LOVING
AND
LIKING

I will reveal to you a love potion, without medicine, without herbs, without any witch's magic; if you want to be loved then love.

Hecaton of Rhodes,
in Seneca's Letters from a Stoic

In as much as love grows in you,
so in you beauty grows.
For love is the beauty of the soul.

St Augustine

'To be in love with oneself is the beginning of a lifelong romance.' To that I add: 'and in every way more satisfactory, and safer.'

A.L. Rowse,
Portrait and Views

Life is so short and death so certain, and when death comes, the silence and separation are so complete, that one can never make too much of the ties and affections and relationships which bind us to the living.

Marie Belloc Lowndes

I have often thought, that as longevity is generally desired, and I believe, generally expected, it would be wise to be continually adding to the number of our friends, that the loss of some may be supplied by others. Friendship, 'the wine of life', should, like a well-stocked cellar, be thus continually renewed; and it is consolatory to think, that although we can seldom add what will equal the generous first growths of our youth, yet friendship becomes insensibly old in much less time than is commonly imagined, and not many years are required to make it very mellow and pleasant.

James Boswell,
Life of Johnson

I have had the rarest, the finest friends. I have loved my friends; the rarest wits of my generation were my boon companions; everything conspired to enable me to gratify my body and my brain; and do you think this would have been so if I had been a good man? If you do you are a fool; good intentions and bald greed go to the wall, but subtle selfishness with a dash of unscrupulousness pulls more plums out of life's pie than the seven deadly virtues. If you are a good man you want a bad one to convert; if you are a bad man you want a bad one to go out on a spree with.

George Moore,
Conversations in Ebury Street

A great man is one who has not lost his child's heart.

James Legge (Trs.)
The Works of Mencius

Never tell a loved one about an infidelity: you would be badly rewarded for your trouble. Although one dislikes being deceived, one likes even less to be undeceived.

Ninon de Lanclos,
quoted by Lilian Day in
Ninon – A Courtisan of Quality

To be deprived of the person we love is happiness compared to living with one we hate.

You cannot go far in friendship if you are not willing to forgive each other little failings.

J. De La Bruyère,
Characters

Friends are God's apology for relations.

Hugh Kingsmill in Michael Holroyd (Ed.),
The Best of Hugh Kingsmill, Introduction

MAN
AND
WOMAN

Most virtuous women, like hidden treasures, are secure because nobody seeks after them.

> Francois de la Rochefoucauld,
> *Maxims*

Crime is a man's disease.

> Lord Stonham
> (to Miss Foyle)

She never forgot the warning Madame de Chevigne gave her when she was twenty: 'My child, all men are pimps.'

> Edmonde Charles Roux,
> *Chanel and Her World*

Only, that all men are monkeys more or less, or else that you and I should have such baboons as these to choose out of, is a mortifying thing, my dear.

in Samuel Richardson,
Clarissa

An awful lot of women haven't realised what it means to be a woman. There isn't an enormous difference between the characteristics of a man or a woman: they are people who fulfill different functions. I loathe a lot of modern psychology because it has lost touch with common sense. Men get it wrong when they try to be manly; women get it wrong when they try to be feminine – or, for that matter, – 'earth mothers'. Get self-conscious and you become like those hothouse lilies that have been over-bred for so long that they've had the scent bred right out of them. Being a woman is being positive, natural, and not losing your instinctive, intuitive self.

Jean Muir
(in a newspaper interview)

It is remarkable that, with theorists of this class, it is not the amount of toil, crushing alike to brain and body, which the female undertakes that is objected to; it is the form and the amount of the reward. It is not the hand-labouring woman, even in his own society, worn out and prematurely aged at forty by domestic work that has no beginning and knows no end, nor the haggard, work-crushed woman and mother who irons his shirts, nor the potential mother who destroys health and youth in the sweater's den where she sews the garments in which he appears so radiantly in the drawing room, which disturbs him. It is the thought of the female doctor with an income of some hundreds a year, who drives round in her carriage to see her patients, or receives them in her consulting-rooms, and who spends the evening smoking and reading before her study fire or entertains guests; it is the thought of the woman who, as legislator, may loll for perhaps six hours of the day on the padded seat of the assembly bench, relieving the tedium now and then by a turn in the refreshment-room, when she is not needed to vote or speak; it is the thought of the woman as Greek professor, with three or four hundred a year, who gives half a dozen lectures a week and has leisure to enjoy the society of her husband and children, and to devote to her own study and life of thought; it is she who wrings his heart! It is not the woman, who, on hands and knees scrubs the floors of the public buildings, or private dwellings, that fills him with anguish for womanhood. That 'quadrupedal' posture is for him, 'truly feminine', and does not interfere with his ideal of the mother and child-bearer.

Olive Schreiner,
Woman and Labour

She was in daily contact with him at the Court, and she studied him with those quick critical eyes of a clever woman, the most unerring things in life when they are not blinded by love.

Conan Doyle

It has been observed that women have more tact, and insight into character than men, that they find out a pedant, a pretender, a blockhead, sooner. The explanation is, that they trust more to the first impressions and natural indications of things, without troubling themselves with a learned theory of them; whereas men, affecting greater gravity, and thinking themselves bound to justify their opinions, are afraid to form any judgement at all, without the formality of proofs and definitions, and blunt the edge of their understandings, lest they should commit some mistake. They stay for facts, till it is too late to pronounce on the characters. Women are naturally physiognomists, and men phrenologists. The first judge by sensations; the last by rules.

William Hazlitt

Our aunts and grandmothers always tell us men are a
sort of animal, that if ever they are constant 'tis only
where they are ill used.

Lady Wortley Montagu,
Complete Letters

'One day my secretary came to me', she begins in a
quavering voice, 'and said "Something very peculiar is
happening". I looked down and saw a policeman
standing on the patio of the Iranian Embassy – that one,
there.' She indicates a house on the end. 'He was
pointing a revolver at the window and there was a black
man with a gun pointing it at the policeman. It was
hideous. It was the siege of the embassy that you must
have read about. Men were rushing about with guns.
Well, the two of us, when we put our heads out of the
window and realised it was a shoot-out, immediately
said, "Oh, men!" That's the sort of remark that justifies
the statement that men and women don't like each
other.'

Dame Rebecca West
(in a newspaper interview)

He gave up his former courses, and took a wife, Fulvia, the widow of Clodius, the demagogue, a woman not born for spinning or housewifery, nor one that could be content with ruling a private husband, but prepared to govern a first magistrate, or give orders to a commander-in-chief. So that Cleopatra had great obligations to her for having taught Antony to be so good a servant, he coming to her hands tame and broken into entire obedience to the commands of the mistress. He used to play all sorts of sportive, boyish tricks, to keep Fulvia in good humour.

Plutarch,
Life of Antony

One of the reasons I don't see eye to eye with Women's Lib is that women have it all on a plate if only they knew it. They don't have to be pretty either.

Charlotte Rampling

SOCIAL GRACES

In the 1920's, girls were more free and bold than they had been – but not as today. Affairs were conducted with discretion: people didn't tell about them. Those who were ten years older than myself were awfully inclined to act the great lady. My mother-in-law, who had been a dancer, at the Alhambra, never gave up looking smart and soignée, even when she was over ninety. Their discipline was fantastic.

Evelyn Laye

On an occasion of less consequence, when he turned his back on Lord Bolingbroke in the rooms at Bright-helmstone, he made this excuse: 'I am not obliged, Sir (said he to Mr Thrale, who stood fretting), to find reasons for respecting the rank of him who will not condescend to declare it by his dress or some visible mark: what are the stars and other signs of superiority made for?'

Hester Lynch Piozzi
Anecdotes of the Late Samuel Johnson

There is one principle of elegance, and the Romans summed it up in one word, decorum. That means what is suitable. Choose what is suitable, Madame, what is suitable to the hour, the circumstances, the temperature, the setting, the landscape, the place you live in, capital, spa, beach resort, or country. Choose with taste what is suitable to your mood, what is most appropriate to your character.

Paul Poiret

One excuse is better than several.

Aldous Huxley

So remember that a good conversationalist is, first and foremost, a good listener. In fact, among people who are widely regarded as great conversationalists, there are some who hardly ever open their mouths at all.

Quentin Crisp and Donald Carroll,
Doing it with Style

I was brought up to contribute my share to conversation at the risk of uttering platitudes, and in China the exchange of platitudes was essential to social intercourse. *Il faut savoir s'ennuyer.*

Harold Acton,
Memoirs of an Aesthete

A gentleman never heard a story before.

Austin O'Malley,
Keystones of Thought

Good manners is the art of making those people easy with whom we converse. Whoever makes the fewest people uneasy is the best bred in the company.

Jonathan Swift, 1720

If a man has good manners and is not afraid of other people, he will get by, even if he is stupid.

Lord Eccles

The great secret, Eliza, is not having bad manners or good manners or any other sort of manners, but having the same manner for all human souls: in short, behaving as if you were in Heaven, where there are no third-class carriages, and one soul is as good as another.

George Bernard Shaw,
Pygmalion

You must always be polite, particularly to those whom you dislike, because politeness is a mark of superiority; and in order to make unpleasant people respect you, you should endeavour to appear as superior to them as possible.

George Bernard Shaw,
My Dear Dorothea

MISFORTUNE

Provided that one's thinking has not been adding anything to it, pain is a trivial sort of thing. If by contrast you start giving yourself encouragement, saying to yourself, 'It's nothing – or nothing much, anyway – let's stick it out, it'll be over presently', then in thinking it a trivial matter you will be ensuring that it actually is. Everything hangs on one's thinking.

Seneca,
Letters from a Stoic

Nothing else in the world can make man unhappy but fear. The misfortune we suffer is seldom if ever as bad as that which we fear.

Schiller

Mishaps are like knives, that either serve us or cut us, as we grip them by the blade or the handle.

James Russell Lowell,
'Cambridge Thirty Years Ago', in *Literary Essays, Vol. 1*

'Are you acquainted with the terrible, the devastating words, if I may call them so, the fiat of Doom: "I don't know if you know, Sir?" As when the housemaid comes into your bedroom in the morning and says: "I don't know if you know, Sir, that the bath has fallen through the kitchen ceiling!" '

Henry James

'Consider, Sir, how insignificant this will appear a twelvemonth hence.' – Were this consideration to be applied to most of the little vexatious incidents of life, by which our quiet is too often disturbed, it would prevent many painful sensations.

James Boswell,
Life of Johnson

He that wrestles with us strengthens our nerves and sharpens our skill. Our antagonist is our helper.

Edmund Burke,
Reflections on the Revolution in France

MORTALITY
AND
ENDURANCE

It is wonderful to be young, but a great relief to be old. So little is expected of the ancient person. Business worries recede. No more tiring parties, you may wear what you like, you may say what you like, you may almost commit any crime you like.

To be forgiven everything and to want almost nothing. To live quietly, with the people and books you love, is the nearest thing to heaven that one hopes one is approaching – given good health and a quiet mind.

Christina Foyle would be grateful to hear from anyone who can identify the above quotation.

Past happiness is not past if its memory is still fragrant. I would give all my future – to be sure there is not much of it in store for me – for the lovely and gracious past, though it be but a memory.

W. Graham Robertson,
Time Was

The Scythians always ate their grandfathers; they be-
haved very respectfully to them for a long time, but as
soon as their grandfathers became old and troublesome,
and began to tell long stories, they immediately ate
them. Nothing could be more improper, and even
disrespectful, than dining off such near and venerable
relations; yet we could not with any propriety accuse
them of bad taste in morals.

Sydney Smith,
in Hesketh Pearson, *Smith of Smiths*

We all live the longer, at least the happier, for having
things our own way; this is my conjugal maxim. I own
'tis not the best of maxims, but I maintain 'tis not the
worst.

Sterne's Letters – 20.1.1764

There is one thing to be thankful for – I shall never be
young again.

Byron's
Claire Clairmont and Lord Berners

When we hear that memory has gone as age has come on, we should understand that the capacity for interest in the matter concerned has perished. A man will be generally very old and feeble before he forgets how much money he has in the funds.

Anthony Trollope,
Autobiography

'There are many virtues in growing old.' He paused, he swallowed, he wet his lips, he looked about. The pause stretched out, he looked dumbstruck. The pause became too long – far too long. He looked down, studying the table top. A terrible tremor of nervousness went through the room. Was he ill? Would he ever be able to get on with it? Finally he looked up and said, 'I'm just trying to think what they are!'

Somerset Maugham

What is the good of getting old, if you don't get artful.

My taxi driver

Yes! It was the one instance Marius, always eagerly on the look-out for such, had yet seen of a perfectly tolerable, perfectly beautiful old age – an old age in which there seemed, to one who perhaps habitually over-valued the expression of youth, nothing to be regretted, nothing really lost, in what years had been taken away. The wise old man, whose blue eyes and fair skin were so delicate, uncontaminate, and clear, would seem to have replaced carefully and consciously each natural trait of youth, and had the blitheness, the placid cheerfulness, as he had also the infirmity, the claim on stronger people, of a delighted child.

Walter Pater,
Marius the Epicurean

In old age, elegance and fastidiousness are a form of dignity.

Coco Chanel,
in Claude Baillen, *Chanel Solitaire*

In spite of illness, in spite of the arch-enemy sorrow, one *can* remain alive long past the usual date of disintegration if one is not afraid of change, insatiable in intellectual curiosity, interested in big things, and happy in small ways.

Edith Wharton,
A Backward Glance

Only one principle will give you courage. That is the principle that no evil lasts forever, nor indeed for very long.

Epicurus,
Morals

From too much love of living,
From hope and fear set free,
We thank with brief thanksgiving
Whatever gods may be
That no man lives for ever,
That dead men rise up never,
That even the weariest river
Winds somewhere safe to sea.

Algernon Charles Swinburne,
'Swan Song', from *The Garden of Proserpine*

ACKNOWLEDGEMENTS

Acknowledgement is made for the reproduction of material to:

W.H. Allen (for Margot Fonteyn), Allen and Unwin (for Bertrand Russell, Arnold Bennett), Allison and Busby (for Kay Dick), Jonathan Cape (for André Maurois, Field Marshal Wavell), Chatto and Windus (for James Lees Milne, Percy Muir, W.S. Gilbert, Compton Mackenzie), Collier Macmillan (for Moreau), William Collins (for Claude Baillen, T.H. White), Constable (for Logan Pearsall Smith, St John Ervine, George Bernard Shaw), Coronet (for Robert Townsend), Dent (for Francis Bacon, Robert Burton, Samuel Richardson, Samuel Butler, Charles Dickens) Devin Aclair (for Austin O'Malley), Eyre Methuen (for Quentin Crisp and Donald Carroll), Fontana (for Roland H. Bainton), Gollancz (for Michael Holroyd), Greenwood Press (for Benjamin Franklin), Gregg International (for Astolphe de Custine), Hamish Hamilton (for Hesketh Pearson, Lucy Norton, Frank Swinnerton), Harvester Press (for George Gissing), Heinemann (for George Moore, Elsie de Wolfe, Lord Brabazon, Pluto, Plutarch), Hodder and Stoughton (for Cecil Roberts), Hutchinson (for J.E. Morpurgo), Jarrolds (for Lillian Day), Macdonald (for Bette Davis), Macmillan (for Walter Pater, A.L. Rowse),

Methuen (for G.K Chesterton, Harold Acton, Hesketh Pearson [Dizzy]), Millington (for Francois de la Rochefoucauld), John Murray (for Iris Origo), Oxford University Press (for Anthony Trollope, William Cobbett, Benjamin Disraeli, Lady Wortley Montagu, Hesther Lynch Piozzi, James Boswell), Penguin (for E.M. Forster, Michel de Montaigne, Lao-Tzu, Wordsworth, Erasmus, Confucius, Seneca, James Legge, J. de la Bruyere, Edmund Burke), Quartet (for W. Graham Robertson), Secker and Warburg (for Arthur Machen, Phylis McGinley), Star Books (for Paul Getty), Weidenfeld and Nicolson (for Cecil Beaton, Edmonde Charles Roux).

I apologise for any inadvertent omissions of acknowledgement for other passages quoted.

C.F.